flowe

flo flip

a guide to 50 favorite flowers

from Florists' Review Enterprises

ISBN 978-0-9801815-6-2

9 780980 181562 51295

waxflower

wax•flow•er

botanical name:
Chamelaucium spp.

how to say it:
kam-e-LAW-see-um

common names:
Waxflower, Geraldton waxflower

what they look like

Waxflowers' small waxy blooms, which are composed of five roundish petals surrounding a nectar cup, occur in airy sprays on branching woody stems that have narrow needlelike leaves.

colors

Pink, rose, mauve, red-violet, lavender, purple, white and cream

special care

FLOWER AND LEAF ISSUES The most common post-harvest problems are bloom and bud drop, drying out of blooms and buds, and premature leaf yellowing.

Causes include *Botrytis* (gray mold) and exposure to ethylene, both of which commonly occur during transport and storage. Water stress (dehydration) also can cause these problems.

To reduce the possibility of *Botrytis* at the retail level, remove any stem ties, and loosen bunches to increase air circulation between stems. To reduce the effects of exposure to ethylene, make sure your purchases are treated with an ethylene inhibitor at the grower level or during shipping.

ETHYLENE SENSITIVE Yes

vase life

Average

did you know

Native to Western Australia, waxflowers contain an aromatic oil; when leaves, blooms and stems are crushed, they emit a pleasing citrus aroma.

general care for most flowers

step 1 When flowers arrive in your store, immediately check the temperature inside the boxes or wet packs with a needle thermometer. (Insert the probe through the side of the boxes behind the flower heads or into the water of Procona or other wet packs.) If temperatures are higher than 40 F, closely examine flowers for *Botrytis* (gray mold); yellowed leaves; and loss of flowers, buds and leaves.

step 2 Unpack flowers immediately, and carefully remove any bunch bindings. Leaving sleeves on at this point can help prevent damage to some blooms, but remove the sleeves eventually to promote air circulation among the blooms.

step 3 Remove all leaves that would be under water in storage containers, and rinse stem ends under tepid running water.

step 4 Recut the stems, on an angle, either under water or in air, with a sharp knife or pruner, removing *at least* 1 inch from the stem ends.

step 5 Dip or place the stem ends into a hydration solution, then place the stems into a clean container partially filled with lukewarm (100 F to 110 F) properly proportioned flower-food solution.

step 6 Place flowers immediately into a floral cooler at 33 F to 35 F and 85 percent to 90 percent humidity for at least two hours before designing with or selling them.

key to "Vase Life"

short	Up to five days
average	Six to 10 days
long	More than 10 days

flower•flip
from Florists' Review Enterprises
www.floristsreview.com
www.superfloralretailing.com
800.367.4708

tulip

tu • lip

botanical name:
Tulipa spp.

how to say it:
TOO-li-pa

common name:
Tulip

what they look like

These goblet-shaped flowers are classified into 15 divisions based on the form of the blooms. Those most commonly grown as cut flowers are single, double (peony flowered), parrot (ruffled and multicolored), lily flowered (pointed petals) and fringed (serrated petal edges).

colors

Red, pink, orange, peach, salmon, apricot, yellow, purple, lavender, white and bicolors

did you know

Tulip stems (scapes) often continue to elongate after they're cut and after they're arranged, so place them deeper into arrangements than where you want them to be.

special care

THE RIGHT FOOD AND WATER Store and arrange tulips in bulb-flower-food solution prepared with cold nonfluoridated water.
CURVACEOUS FLOWERS Tulips are geotropic (affected by gravity) and phototropic (curve toward the light), so store them upright in their containers and in a dark area of the cooler where they're shielded from the light (unless the light source is from directly above the flowers). Some care experts recommend leaving tulips in their sleeves during storage to help prevent stem curving.
ETHYLENE SENSITIVE No

vase life

Short

agapanthus

ag•a•pan•thus

botanical name:
Agapanthus africanus
how to say it:
ag-uh-PAN-thus af-ri-KAW-nus
common names:
Lily-of-the-Nile, African lily

what they look like

Spherical flower heads are made up of clusters of small six-petaled funnel-shaped blooms (20 to 50) atop tall, smooth leafless stems.

colors

Pale blue to dark blue and white

vase life

Average

did you know

Standard *Agapanthuses* grow as tall as 3 feet, with flower heads as large as 6 inches in diameter; however, miniature varieties also are available.

special care

FLOWER FOOD Research shows that *Agapanthuses* receive little benefit from the nutrient (sugar) in flower-food solutions; however, you should still use flower-food solution in storage and arrangement containers to control bacterial growth. And because these flowers are grown from rhizomes, you can use flower food formulated for bulb flowers.

BLOOM DROP Loss of flower buds and florets indicates exposure to ethylene gas, so make sure your purchases are treated with an ethylene inhibitor at the grower level or during transportation, and keep them away from sources of ethylene in your store, especially fruit.

ETHYLENE SENSITIVE Yes

sunflower

sun•flow•er

botanical name:
Helianthus annuus

how to say it:
hee-lee-AN-thus AN-yoo-us

common name:
Sunflower

what they look like

Sunflowers have nodding daisylike blossoms that can be 2 to 10 or more inches in diameter, depending on the variety. The petals (ray florets) on most varieties surround yellow, brown, green or deep purple centers (disk florets), although some varieties appear not to have center disks.

colors

Yellow, bronze, brown, reddish-brown, orange, cream and bicolors. Stem-dyed sunflowers (red and orange) have grown in popularity recently.

did you know

Sunflowers are native to the Americas, from southern Canada to South America, and they were first domesticated in Mexico.

special care

PROCESS IMMEDIATELY Sunflowers are highly susceptible to water stress, so remove them from the shipping boxes immediately upon their arrival. Because they are often field grown and have "hairy" stems, they capture debris, so rinse the stems under tepid running water.

KEEP THEM VERTICAL Sunflowers are geotropic (affected by the force of gravity), so store them as vertical as possible, particularly at room temperatures, so their heads won't nod even more than they already do.

ETHYLENE SENSITIVE Yes

vase life

Average

allium

al•li•um

botanical name:
Allium spp.
how to say it:
AL-ee-um
common names:
Onion, Flowering onion, Ornamental onion (also Garlic, Leek, Chive)

what they look like

Some species have spherical flower heads (1 inch to 6 inches in diameter) made up of dense clusters of tiny blooms (dozens to hundreds of blooms) atop tall, smooth leafless stems. Other species have much less dense and looser flower heads with fewer florets.

colors

Purple, lavender, red-violet, mauve, yellow and white

did you know

Edible parts of *Alliums* vary by species: Edible bulbs include onions, scallions, shallots and garlic; edible leaves include chives; and edible stems include leeks.

special care

FLOWER FOOD *Alliums* are bulb flowers, so use flower food formulated for bulb flowers in storage and arrangement containers.

RESHAPING BLOOMS *Alliums* should be purchased with about 30 percent of their blooms open. During shipping, the dense spherical flower heads often become smashed, but the perfect roundness can be restored by rolling each stem back and forth between the palms of your hands.

ETHYLENE SENSITIVE Yes

vase life

Average

stock

stock

botanical name:
Matthiola incana

how to say it:
maw-tee-OH-la in-KAY-na

common names:
Stock, Gillyflower

what they look like

Stocks have dense columnar clusters of blooms that are about 1 inch in diameter. Both single and double flower forms exist, but the double forms are the most desirable. The flowers have a strong spicy clovelike fragrance.

colors

Purple, lavender, red-violet, red, pink, peach, pale yellow, cream and white

vase life

Average

did you know

Stocks are a member of the mustard *(Cruciferae)* family and are related to radish, horseradish, turnip, rutabaga, cabbage, kale, broccoli and watercress.

special care

THE KINDEST CUTS When recutting the stems during processing, remove all portions of stem ends that are semiwoody, whitish and/or root bearing. Do not smash or crush the stem ends; doing so will damage the stems' vascular system.

ROOM TO BREATHE To help prevent the development of gray mold *(Botrytis)* on the flower spikes and leaves, do not pack stocks tightly in storage containers, ensuring that air will circulate adequately.

FREQUENT MAINTENANCE Clean storage containers, change the flower-food solution, and rinse and recut stems at least every other day because stocks can quickly create an unpleasant smell.

ETHYLENE SENSITIVE Yes

alstroemeria

al•stroe•me•ri•a

botanical name:
Alstroemeria, Dutch hybrids

how to say it:
al-stro-MEE-ree-uh

common names:
Peruvian lily, Lily-of-the-Incas

what they look like

Alstroemerias' six-"petaled" trumpet-shaped blooms, often spotted or streaked, resemble miniature lilies and appear individually on lateral branchlets clustered atop smooth stems that bear scattered thin twisted leaves.

colors

Solid colors and bicolors, in virtually every hue except blue-green and blue

vase life

Long

did you know

Frequent handling of *Alstroemerias* can cause an inflammation of the skin (contact dermatitis/allergic dermatitis) in some people. Those people should wear latex gloves when handling these flowers.

special care

KEEPING LEAVES GREEN *Alstroemeria* foliage can turn yellow quickly. Using pretreatments formulated specifically for *Alstroemerias* and lilies, as well as "low-dose" (low sugar) flower foods or flower foods formulated especially for bulb flowers, can decrease premature leaf yellowing.

TRIMMING STEMS When recutting stems, remove any whitish, or "blanched," portion at the bottoms of the stems to enhance the uptake of flower-food solution.

STIMULATING LIFE Removal of buds from the base of the first open flower will increase vase life and promote the development of the other flowers.

ETHYLENE SENSITIVE Yes

star-of-bethlehem

star-of-beth•le•hem

botanical name:
Ornithogalum spp.

how to say it:
or-ni-THOG-uh-lum

common names:
Star-of-Bethlehem, Chincherinchee

what they look like

Depending on species, *Ornithogalums* have spiked or round clusters of star-shaped, sometimes fragrant blooms atop smooth, leafless stems.

colors

White to ivory and golden-yellow to orange

vase life

Long

did you know

The spiked species of *Ornithogalums* are geotropic (affected by the forces of gravity), are phototropic (curve toward light) and continue to grow (elongate) after they're cut.

special care

BACTERIA CONTROL Some cut flower care and handling authorities suggest that the nutrient (sugar) in fresh flower foods does not affect *Ornithogalums*. However, flower-food solutions should still be used to control microbial growth in storage and arrangement containers, which can plug stem ends and prohibit water uptake.

GROOMING ESSENTIALS Because these flowers have an abundance of individual blossoms that open over time, it is important to remove blooms as they fade to keep the flower heads looking their best throughout these flowers' long lives.

ETHYLENE SENSITIVE No

amaryllis

am•a•ryl•lis

botanical name:
Hippeastrum spp.

how to say it:
hip-ee-AS-trum

common names:
Amaryllis, Barbados lily

what they look like

Amaryllises' showy blooms are trumpet shaped and range from 3 to 8 inches in diameter. There are generally three to five blooms atop each stem. The blooms can be single, double or triple flowered.

colors

Red, pink, red-orange, orange, peach, salmon, yellow, green, white and bicolors

vase life

Average

special care

STORAGE TEMPS Amaryllises are tropical bulb flowers, so they prefer refrigeration at temperatures between 41 F and 50 F. If open blooms are needed quickly, store these flowers out of the cooler, at room temperature.

AVOID SPLIT ENDS Amaryllis stem ends are prone to splitting and curling. Help prevent this by wrapping the bases of the stems with waterproof tape.

ETHYLENE SENSITIVE Yes

did you know

Amaryllises are one of the few tropical bulb flowers. They are native to the Caribbean region and to tropical and subtropical South America (Peru, Brazil, Bolivia, Chile and Argentina).

solidago

sol•i•da•go

botanical name:
Solidago spp.

how to say it:
saul-i-DAY-go

common name:
Goldenrod

what they look like

Solidago has pyramidal clusters of tiny flowers in branched, arched plumes. Tall, stiff thin stems have elliptic to lance-shaped leaves, the longest of which occur in the middle of the stems.

colors

Yellow, golden yellow

vase life

Average

did you know

Contrary to popular belief, goldenrod *(Solidago)* is not allergenic; its pollen is heavy and cannot be carried easily by wind. Ragweed *(Ambrosia)* pollen, which is light and wind-borne, is the most common cause of allergic reactions (hay fever).

special care

LEAF YELLOWING AND REMOVAL

Solidago foliage often turns yellow quickly; this is normal, and there is little that can be done about it at the retail level. It is important, though, to leave foliage on the stems (above water only) during storage; remove the leaves just prior to arranging these flowers.

FRESH TO DRY *Solidago* can be air dried when the flowers are in a healthy stage. Tie several stems in a bunch, and hang them upside down in a dry, airy, dark room until they're dried. The temperature in the room can be either warm or cool.

ETHYLENE SENSITIVE No

anemone

a•nem•o•ne

botanical name:
Anemone coronaria
how to say it:
uh-NEM-oh-nee kor-oh-NAW-ree-uh
common names:
Windflower, Wind poppy

what they look like

Anemones have cup-shaped, poppylike blooms that can open to about 2 to 3 inches in diameter. There are single, semidouble and double forms. Stems are leafless.

colors

Pink, red, mauve, purple and blue-violet, with black centers
White, with yellow or neutral centers

vase life

Short

did you know

Anemones have no true petals; what appear to be petals are really sepals, which have assumed the coloring and characteristics of petals.

special care

FLOWER FOOD Some research indicates that *Anemones* receive little benefit from the nutrient (sugar) in flower-food solutions; however, you should still use flower-food solution in storage and arrangement containers to control bacterial growth. And because these flowers are grown from tubers, you can use flower food formulated for bulb flowers.

STEM STRAIGHTENING Keep *Anemones* in their sleeves during processing and hydration to help keep their stems straight.

ETHYLENE SENSITIVE Yes

snapdragon

snap•drag•on

botanical name:
Antirrhinum majus

how to say it:
an-ti-RYE-num MAY-jus

common name:
Snapdragon

what they look like

Snapdragons are spike flowers, with small florets occurring on the upper portions of tall, thin leafy stems. These flowers get their common name because the individual florets each resemble a dragon's mouth.

colors

Red, burgundy, magenta, pink, orange, peach, salmon, yellow, purple, lavender, white, ivory and bicolors

vase life

Average

did you know

You can entertain customers and children by gently squeezing the sides of a floret, which opens and closes the "dragon's mouth."

special care

LEAVE THE LIGHTS ON When storing snapdragons, leave the lights on in your cooler, or the colors may fade dramatically.

KEEP THEM VERTICAL Snapdragons are geotropic (affected by the force of gravity), and the tips of the flower spikes will curve upwards if the stems are laid horizontally or placed at an angle in containers—so always store them vertically in tall buckets.

LEAVE LEAVES Do not remove more foliage than necessary (only leaves that would be under water in storage containers) because this can stimulate flower drop.

ETHYLENE SENSITIVE Yes

anthurium

an•thu•ri•um

botanical name:
Anthurium spp.

how to say it:
an-THOO-ree-um

common names:
Tailflower, Flamingo flower

what they look like

"Blooms" consist of a flat heart-shaped colored spathe, from which protrudes a fingerlike spadix (the true flower head). Stems are thin, smooth and leafless.

colors

Red, pink, burgundy, red-orange, orange, peach, salmon, brown, rust, green, lavender, white and ivory, as well as bicolors *(obake)*, one color of which is usually green

vase life

Long

did you know

The fingerlike spadix is the true flower head (inflorescence), and the "bumps" on the spadix are the real flowers. The number of open flowers determines the roughness of the spadix.

special care

STORAGE TEMPS *Anthuriums* are tropical flowers and, therefore, are chill sensitive. Store them at 55 F to 65 F. If *Anthuriums* are subjected to temperatures lower than 50 F for extended periods, including during shipping, the spathes will turn bluish-purple, gray or black, and the spadices will turn brown and wilt.

DUNKING FLOWERS If *Anthuriums* arrive dehydrated and wilty, submerge the flowers (flower heads and stems) in room-temperature water for two or more hours. Recut stems while they are submerged.

STEM BLOCKAGE *Anthuriums* are highly susceptible to stem blockage by microbes, so recut the stem ends and change flower-food solution at least every other day.

ETHYLENE SENSITIVE No

rose

rose

botanical name:
Rosa spp.
how to say it:
ROW-za
common name:
Rose

classifications of hybrids:

- Hybrid tea rose (classic long-stemmed roses)
- Garden rose / English rose
- Spray rose / Sweetheart rose / Intermediate rose

what they look like

Hybrid tea rose blooms range from cup shaped to tulip shaped. Garden rose blooms are larger and more peonylike. Spray, sweetheart and intermediate rose blooms are smaller, and spray roses have multiple blooms on branched stems.

colors

Solid colors and bicolors in virtually every hue except blue-green and blue

vase life

Average

did you know

The life expectancy of cut roses varies dramatically among varieties and is strongly influenced by their growing environment and the shipping and handling methods employed from farm to florist.

special care

KEEP COLD AND HYDRATED Roses require cold (33 F to 35 F), humid (85 percent to 90 percent humidity) environments with circulating air. They also require lots of water. Room temperatures and water deprivation can result in reduced vase life; fungus and gray mold *(Botrytis)* on petals, leaves, and stems; and flowers that open too quickly or fail to open at all.

NOURISH PROPERLY Store and arrange roses in a flower-food solution specifically formulated for roses. When properly used, it can double vase life, reduce bent neck, prevent petal drop and slow color fading.

ETHYLENE SENSITIVE Yes

baby's breath

ba•by's breath

botanical name:
Gypsophila paniculata
how to say it:
jip-SOF-il-uh pan-ik-you-LAW-tuh
common name:
Baby's breath

what they look like

Small, dainty flowers, on delicate stems, occur in branched clusters (panicles) at stem ends. Bloom sizes and density vary by cultivar, and flower forms include singles, doubles and semidoubles. Sparse, tiny foliage appears at nodes on main stems.

colors

White and pale pink.

vase life

Average

did you know

You can speed the opening of the blooms by rapidly "shaking" the stems of the bunches up and down in a container of warm water. Florets will pop open like miniature popcorn.

special care

BEWARE OF ETHYLENE *Gypsophila* is extremely sensitive to ethylene, which accelerates wilting and causes translucent blooms. Make sure your purchases are treated with an ethylene inhibitor at the grower level or during transportation, and keep them away from sources of ethylene in your store such as fruit and decaying flowers and foliage.

SOLUTION CONTAMINATION Storage solution can quickly become contaminated and smelly, so change it and recut flower stems at least every other day. Some experts recommend adding one teaspoon of chlorine bleach to every gallon of flower-food solution.

ETHYLENE SENSITIVE Yes

ranunculus

ra•nun•cu•lus

botanical name:
Ranunculus asiaticus

how to say it:
ran-NUN-cue-lus ay-see-AT-i-kus

common name:
Persian buttercup

what they look like

Ranunculi have cup-shaped or bowl-shaped blooms, in single- or double-flowered forms. Most cut flower varieties are doubles, having multiple layers of petals—which are sometimes papery looking—and resembling small peonies. Stems are hollow and brittle and sport double- or triple-segmented leaves.

colors

Red, rose, pink, orange, yellow and white, as well as bicolors

did you know

Compounds found in *Ranunculi* are used in the naturopathic treatment of arthritis, sciatica, rheumatism and various skin conditions.

special care

QUICK SALE *Ranunculi* are sensitive to warm environments, but they don't store well in floral coolers. It is best to hold them for no more than two days, at 33 F to 38 F, so avoid purchasing larger quantities than immediately needed.

STRAIGHT TALK To help keep the narrow stems straight, hydrate these flowers in their sleeves for at least one hour before removing the sleeves or refrigerating the flowers. You also can strengthen them by inserting enameled wire or chenille stems into the hollow stems when designing.

ETHYLENE SENSITIVE Yes

vase life

Short

banksia

bank•si•a

botanical name:
Banksia spp.

how to say it:
BANK-see-uh

common name:
Australian honeysuckle is the generic common name for all *Banksias*; however, each species has a unique common name.

what they look like

Banksias have large cylindrical, round or acorn-shaped flower heads that are tightly packed with small flowers. Leaves are generally narrow, long and stiff, with finely serrated to jaggedly saw-toothed edges. Stems are thick and woody.

colors

Red, orange, yellow, gold, green and earth tones (tans).

vase life

Long

did you know

The colors of some species and varieties of *Banksias* change over time in vase solutions. This natural phenomenon is only partially related to aging.

special care

WET ROT Because of the density of the tiny flowers on the flower heads, *Banksias* can rot easily if they get wet, so ensure the flower heads stay dry.

STORAGE TEMPS Although *Banksias* are native to subtropical Australia and South Africa, they are not chill sensitive and can be refrigerated at 33 F to 38 F. Some experts recommend higher storage temperatures, but there is little scientific data to support that recommendation.

FRESH TO DRY *Banksias* are suitable for air drying. Stand the flowers upright in a container or hang them upside down, individually, in a cool, dry, airy, dark room until they are dried.

ETHYLENE SENSITIVE No

queen anne's lace

queen anne's lace

botanical name:
Ammi majus

how to say it:
AM-mee MAY-jus

common names:
Bishop's weed, False Queen Anne's lace

what they look like

Queen Anne's lace has masses of tiny white flowers atop long, thin ferny-leaved stems. The flower heads have a lacy appearance.

colors

White; green and greenish-white varieties have been introduced.

special care

KEEP COLD AND HYDRATED When these flowers are displayed in warm, dry environments, the tiny blooms tend to drop quickly, so continuously store them in a flower cooler at 33 F to 40 F, with 90 percent humidity, until they are sold or ready for delivery.

Recut stems and change flower-food solution at least every other day to reduce bacteria growth and keep solution flowing up the stems.

ETHYLENE SENSITIVE Yes

vase life

Short

did you know

In the commercial floral industry, *Ammi majus* is commonly, but incorrectly, called Queen Anne's lace—which is the common name of a close relative, *Daucus carota*. *D. carota*, also known as "wild carrot," is not cultivated as a cut flower but is often found growing abundantly along roadsides and riverbanks and in fields and wetlands during the summer.

bells-of-ireland

bells-of-ire•land

botanical name:
Moluccella laevis

how to say it:
mow-loo-SELL-uh LAY-vis

common names:
Bells-of-Ireland, Shellflower

what they look like

Bells-of-Ireland are tall "spike" flowers consisting of apple-green bell-shaped (or shell-shaped) calyces that grow in circular clusters (whorls) of six around the upper portion of each stem. The actual flowers are the tiny white blooms inside the calyces.

color

Apple-green

vase life

Average

did you know

Bells-of-Ireland, which are often mistaken as a foliage, are one of the few true green flowers. And despite the common name, they are native to Turkey and Syria.

special care

CURVED TIPS Place bells-of-Ireland stems vertically in their storage containers to prevent stem tips from curving. These flowers are geotropic, meaning they respond to the force of gravity, so when they're stored or arranged diagonally or horizontally, the tips of the flowers will curve upward.

TURNING COLORS Bells-of-Ireland can last up to 10 days, but individual calyces (bells) often start fading earlier. Remove calyces as they fade—unless you eventually want to dry the flowers, which you can do by hanging them upside down in a cool, dry, airy, dark room for several days.

ETHYLENE SENSITIVE No

protea

pro•te•a

botanical name:
Protea spp.

how to say it:
PRO-tee-uh, pro-TEE-uh

common name:
Sugarbush is the generic common name for all *Proteas*; however, each species has a unique common name.

what they look like

Proteas generally have dome- or cone-shaped flower heads, about 4 to 12 inches in diameter and 4 to 6 inches in height. The flower heads have dense central masses of "hairy," "furry" or "feathery" flowers surrounded by stiff colored bracts, which, depending on species, also can be hairy, furry or feathery. Stems are woody and crowded with leathery leaves of various forms, which can enshroud the flower heads.

vase life

Long

did you know

Proteas are one of the few flowers pollinated by birds, which produces large amounts of nectar. This is the origin of the common name sugarbush.

colors

Red, burgundy, rose, pink, green and white, with burgundy, pink or white centers and, on some species, black or silvery pubescence (fine, short hairs) on bract edges

special care

NUTRIENTS, TEMPS AND LIGHT Leaf blackening is a common problem. Causes include lack of carbohydrates, not enough light, too warm environments and moisture on leaves. To prevent this problem, use flower foods in proper concentrations; provide plenty of light, even during storage; refrigerate flowers at 33 F to 36 F; and keep leaves dry. Although they are native to tropical and subtropical regions of Africa, *Proteas* are not chill sensitive.

ETHYLENE SENSITIVE No

billy button

bil•ly but•ton

botanical name:
Craspedia globosa

how to say it:
cras-PEE-dee-uh glow-BO-suh

common names:
Billy button, Billy ball, Drumstick, Woollyhead

what they look like

Billy buttons have spherical flower heads (glomerules), 1 inch to 2 inches in diameter, formed of a massive aggregation of tiny flowers, atop long thin leafless stems.

color

Yellow

vase life

Average

did you know

These peculiar flowers, which are native to Australia, New Zealand and Tasmania, are members of the *Compositae* (daisy/sunflower) family, and resemble the center disks of those flowers (without the petals [ray flowers])—only in globular form.

special care

FLORET OPENING The use of flower foods will promote the opening of the tiny florets on the spherical flower heads. This is especially important with flowers that are harvested in a tight, or immature, stage.

FRESH TO DRY Billy buttons are excellent candidates for air drying; they can maintain their color for up to a year. Tie several stems in a bunch, and hang them upside down in a warm, dry, airy, dark room until they're dried.

ETHYLENE SENSITIVE No

peony

pe•o•ny

botanical name:
Paeonia spp.

how to say it:
pee-OWN-ee-uh

common name:
Peony

what they look like

Peony blooms are large—often up to 6 inches in diameter—and have tissuelike petals. Flower forms include single, double, semidouble, Japanese and anemone. Many peony varieties emanate delightful scents.

colors

Pink, red, lavender, purple, salmon, apricot, yellow, cream, white and bicolors

vase life

Short

did you know

Peonies are heavy drinkers, so check their flower-food solution level often, and advise your customers to do so, too.

special care

GET THEM OUT OF THE BOX Immediately remove peonies from the shipping boxes. They are susceptible to *Botrytis* (gray mold), which will rot the flower heads. *Botrytis* loves dark, moist environments, such as inside shipping boxes, and thrives with changes in shipping temperature. Discard any flowers contaminated with *Botrytis*, and notify your supplier.

EXTRA HELP If peonies appear wilted or otherwise water stressed, submerge the entire stems, up to the blooms, into room-temperature water for 20 minutes before processing them. Allow the blooms to dry *thoroughly* before refrigerating them.

ETHYLENE SENSITIVE No

bird-of-paradise

bird-of-par•a•dise

botanical name:
Strelitzia reginae

how to say it:
stre-LITZ-ee-uh ray-JEEN-ee

common names:
Bird-of-paradise, Crane flower

what they look like

The flower head is a boat-shaped bract from which pointed featherlike flowers emerge. Each flower has a blue or purplish structure called a tongue. The bract extends from the top of a smooth leafless stem at an angle (90 degrees or less).

colors

Orange to yellow-orange, with blue/blue-violet tongues. Bracts are grayish green to purplish green and edged in red.

did you know

Birds-of-paradise are one of the few flowers pollinated by birds; however, the common name was given because the open blossoms resemble a crested bird's head or the wings of a bird in flight.

special care

STORAGE TEMPS Birds-of-paradise are subtropical flowers and, therefore, are somewhat chill sensitive. Store them at 45 F to 55. Storage at temperatures lower than 45 F can result in brown lesions on the flowers and bracts and the failure of the flowers to open properly.

MANUALLY OPENING FLOWERS
If flowers fail to emerge from the bract, they can be gently pulled out, one at a time, by hand. Some experts recommend first soaking the flower heads in warm water for 20 minutes or cutting a slit in the bottom of the bract, to make extrication of the flowers easier.

ETHYLENE SENSITIVE No

vase life

Long

orchid

or•chid

botanical names:
Arachnis, Cattleya, Cymbidium, Dendrobium, Mokara, Oncidium, Paphiopedilum, Phalaenopsis, Vanda

how to say them:
uh-RAK-nis, KAT-lee-uh, sim-BID-ee-um, den-DROW-bee-um, mow-KAR-uh, on-SID-ee-um, paf-ee-oh-PED-i-lum, fal-e-NOP-sis, VAN-duh

what they look like

Regardless of type, size or shape of orchid, blooms have six "petals"—actually three sepals, two petals, and a third modified petal that forms a lip.

colors

Vary by genus, but collectively, orchids are available in virtually every hue except blue-green and blue. Most are bicolors, with spots or blotches on lips and/or petals.

special care

STORAGE TEMPS Most types of cut orchids are chill sensitive and should be stored at 55 F to 60 F. *Cymbidium* orchids, however, prefer storage temperatures between 43 F and 55 F.

ANTHER CAUTION Be careful to not damage or remove anther caps (on the center "column" in the "throat") because doing so will hasten the wilting process and stimulate ethylene production.

ETHYLENE SENSITIVE Varies by type. *Cattleyas*, *Cymbidiums* and *Phalaenopses* are moderately to highly sensitive to ethylene while *Dendrobiums* and *Oncidiums* are only slightly or not sensitive.

vase life

Long

did you know

Most of these orchids are "epiphytes," or air plants, that grow on other plants or trees or elevated supports. They obtain water and nutrients from the air. Exceptions are *Cymbidiums* and *Paphiopedilums*, which are "terrestrial" orchids that grow on the ground.

calla

cal•la

botanical name:
Zantedeschia spp.

how to say it:
zan-te-DES-kee-a

common names:
Calla, Miniature calla

what they look like

Callas have funnel-shaped heads and smooth leafless stems. Standard callas have a head size of about 6 inches and stems ranging from 20 to 48 inches. These are largely the white and green-and-white varieties. Miniature callas are the colored callas although there are also white miniature callas. Head sizes range from about 3 to 5 inches and stem lengths from 8 to 32 inches.

colors

White, yellow, orange, pink, red, lavender, purple, green, "black" and bicolors

did you know

Although often called "calla lilies," these flowers are not related to lilies. Instead, they are related to *Anthuriums*, *Caladiums*, *Dieffenbachias* and *Spathiphyllums*.

special care

WATCH THAT CUT When recutting calla stems, avoid removing all of the white stem end, if possible. Leaving part of the white stem ends helps with water uptake and vase life while reducing the chances of stem splitting or curling.

STRAIGHTENING TIP If callas' stems are curved and need to be straightened, wrap them loosely in newspaper, and store them upright in a tall bucket, vase or container.

AVOID SPLIT ENDS Often, the stem ends of callas will split and curl. To minimize this, wrap the stems near their ends with waterproof tape, and don't cut off all of the white portion at the end of the stems.

ETHYLENE SENSITIVE No

vase life

Average

narcissus

nar•cis•sus

botanical name:
Narcissus spp.

how to say it:
nar-SIS-us

common names:
Daffodil, Jonquil, Paper-white

what they look like

All *Narcissus* blooms have petals emanating from the base of a trumpet-shaped cup (corona). Single-flowered varieties have six petals; double-flowered varieties have 12 or more. The blooms are at the tops of stems, and when open, face perpendicular to the stems (approximately 90 degrees). Larger-flowered species sport a single bloom per stem, and smaller-flowered varieties (polyanthus *Narcissi*) sport clusters of blooms per stem.
Stems are hollow and leafless.

did you know

You should sell *Narcissi* (and all spring bulb flowers) within two days of receipt because flowers held for more than two days lose vase life more rapidly than normal at the consumer level.

colors

Yellow, orange, peach, pink, white, cream and greenish petals, with yellow, orange, peach, salmon, pink, white, cream and bicolor cups

special care

TOXIN PROTECTION During processing, isolate *Narcissi* from other flowers because when initially cut, *Narcissi* exude a slimy substance that is harmful to other flowers. Keep *Narcissi* in separate containers for about six hours; after that time, the harmful sap will have leached, and the flowers can be arranged or placed with other flowers, even if recut again, without affecting the lives of the other flowers.

ETHYLENE SENSITIVE Yes

vase life

Short

carnation

car•na•tion

botanical name:
Dianthus caryophyllus

how to say it:
dy-AN-thus care-ee-OFF-i-lus

common names:
Carnation, Clove pink

what they look like

Standard carnations have round, ruffly blossoms that grow up to 3 inches in diameter. Miniature, or spray, carnations' blossoms are usually 1 inch to 2 inches in diameter.

colors

Natural colors include white, ivory, pink, hot pink, red, burgundy, salmon, peach, apricot, orange, yellow, yellow-green, lime green, lavender, purple and bicolors—virtually every color except blue-green and blue.

did you know

Around 90 percent of the carnations sold in the United States today are grown in Colombia.

special care

WATCH OUT FOR ETHYLENE Carnations are highly sensitive to ethylene gas, which accelerates petal wilting. Make sure your purchases are treated with an ethylene inhibitor at the grower level or during transportation. In addition, keep them away from sources of ethylene such as fruit, decaying flowers and foliage, tobacco smoke and automobile exhaust.

BUY THE GRADE YOU NEED Carnations are usually available in various "grades" (e.g., select, fancy, standard, short), which are determined by stem length, strength and straightness; bloom size; and freedom from defects or damage.

vase life

Long

marguerite

mar•gue•rite

botanical name:
Argyranthemum frutescens

how to say it:
ar-gi-RAN-the-mum froo-TESS-enz

common names:
Marguerite, Paris daisy

what they look like

Marguerites are the classic yellow-centered daisies, with a single row of petals (ray flowers) surrounding the centers (disk flowers).

colors

White, yellow and pink

vase life

Average

special care

THE SOLUTION SOLUTION Use only low-dose (low-sugar) flower foods (also known as holding solutions) with marguerites because the nutrient (sugar) provides them little to no benefit—and, in fact, a too-high concentration of sugar can cause the foliage to turn yellow.

FREQUENT MAINTENANCE The solution in which marguerites are held often becomes smelly, so change it at least every other day, and rinse and recut stems and wash containers at that time, as well.

ETHYLENE SENSITIVE No

did you know

Marguerite is the French word for daisy. The origin of the word daisy is Anglo Saxon *daes eage*, meaning day's eye—so called because daisies open at dawn.

china aster

chi•na as•ter

botanical name:
Callistephus chinensis
how to say it:
ka-LIS-te-fuss chin-EN-sis
common names:
China aster, 'Matsumoto' aster, Rainbow aster

what they look like

Blooms can be single, semidouble or double forms and range from about 1 inch to 4 inches in diameter. Some varieties resemble daisies, with yellow centers (disk florets), while others have shaggy plume-like petals (ray florets), with or without exposed centers. Stems are thin, leafy and sometimes branched.

colors

Reds, pinks, violets, lavenders and yellows, from pastel to bright, as well as white, coral and apricot

did you know

'Matsumoto' varieties are among the most prominent China asters. Small-bloomed, branched varieties are often known as rainbow asters.

special care

FOLIAGE ISSUES Leaves often wilt before the flowers completely fade, so consider removing all foliage from the stems when arranging these flowers; however, leave foliage on the upper stems until design time. Also, inform customers of this characteristic.

STEM BLOCKAGE China asters' susceptibility to stem blockage by microbes in flower-food solution is higher than normal, so recut the stem ends and change flower-food solution at least every other day—and advise customers to do the same.

ETHYLENE SENSITIVE No

vase life

Average

lisianthus

lis•i•an•thus

botanical names:
Eustoma, syn. *Lisianthus*

how to say them:
you-STOW-muh, lis-ee-AN-thus

common names:
Prairie gentian, Texas bluebell

what they look like

Single-flowered *Lisianthus* blooms are cup shaped (or tuliplike), and double- and triple-flowered varieties resemble garden roses. The 2-inch-diameter blooms occur at the ends of thin branched stems with gray-green leaves.

colors

White, pastel pink, bright pink, lavender, purple, yellow, salmon/coral and green, as well as bicolors

did you know

Lisianthuses are geotropic (affected by the force of gravity), and their stems will curve upward if stored at an angle (diagonally) or horizontally.

special care

GOOD GROOMING Remove individual blooms as they fade to keep stems and designs looking good and to encourage other buds to open. Buds will often open to a lighter color than the original flowers. Removal of buds can increase the longevity of the main blooms.

DRY AND DISEASE FREE Gray mold *(Botrytis)* can appear as gray patches on leaves, so do not mist these flowers while they're in storage or pack them too tightly in containers, and make sure there is plenty of air circulation among the stems.

ETHYLENE SENSITIVE Yes

vase life

Long

chrysanthemum

chry•san•the•mum

botanical name:
Dendranthema X *grandiflorum*

how to say it:
den-DRAN-thuh-muh grand-i-FLOOR-um

common names:
Chrysanthemum, Mum

what they look like

Chrysanthemums have "composite" flower heads of ray flowers (petal-like florets) and disk flowers (tiny florets in the center) in numerous forms and sizes. There are single-flowered stems (disbuds, standards) and multiflowered stems (sprays). Flower forms include daisy, spider/fuji, cushion, button, spoon-tip/pinwheel, quill-tip and more.

colors

Virtually every hue except blue-green, blue and blue-violet, as well as bicolors

vase life

Long

special care

NO SMASHING Do not smash or break chrysanthemum stem ends; doing so damages the stems and inhibits water uptake. Cut stem ends with a sharp blade, removing any woody portions.

LEAF YELLOWING AND REMOVAL Chrysanthemum foliage can turn yellow prematurely; using flower-food solutions at proper concentrations can help. Leave foliage on the stems (above water) during storage, though; you can remove additional leaves when arranging these flowers.

ETHYLENE SENSITIVE No

did you know

Chrysanthemums originated in China prior to 500 B.C. and were introduced to Japan in A.D. 400, when they became the emblem of the country's imperial family. The Chrysanthemum Throne is the common term for the Imperial Throne of Japan, the oldest monarchy in the world.

limonium

li•mo•ni•um

botanical name:
Limonium spp.
how to say it:
li-MOW-nee-um
common names:
Statice, Sea lavender, Sea-foam statice, Confetti statice, Caspia, German statice

what they look like

There are many species of *Limonium*, but, in general, they have masses of tiny colored papery bracts that surround the true flowers (often white).
The flower clusters are at the ends of multibranched stems.

colors

Purple, lavender, blue-violet, red-violet, pink, peach, salmon, yellow and white

vase life

Long

did you know

The common name "sea lavender" comes from these flowers' native habitats, which are temperate salt-water coastal environments. Statice is an obsolete botanical name.

special care

COLD, MOVING AIR *Botrytis* (gray mold) and yellowing stems and leaves are common problems. To reduce the occurrence of these problems, remove any stem ties and sleeves, and loosen bunches to increase air circulation between stems. Also, recut stems regularly, use flower foods properly and keep flowers refrigerated.

FRESH TO DRY Many species of *Limonium* can be air dried, as long as the flowers are healthy. Tie several stems in a bunch, and hang them upside down in a cool, dry, airy, dark room until they're dried.

ETHYLENE SENSITIVE Yes

dahlia

dahl•ia

botanical name:
Dahlia spp.

how to say it:
DAL-yuh, DOLL-yuh

common name:
None

what they look like

Dahlias are available in diameters ranging from 4 to 12 inches, with one bloom on each leafy stem. The American Dahlia Society has designated 20 classifications of *Dahlias* based on the type and size of their flower heads, including anemone, ball, colarette, decorative, peony, pompon and more.

colors

Virtually every hue except blue-green, blue and blue-violet, as well as bicolors

special care

STORAGE TEMPS *Dahlias* are chill sensitive, so refrigerate them at temperatures between 40 F and 50 F.

BUXOM BLOOMS Some varieties' oversize blossoms may be too heavy for the flowers' hollow stems. When using these large varieties, reinforce the stems with wires or plant stakes, or cut them short for use in compact designs to avoid the appearance of "bent neck."

ETHYLENE SENSITIVE No

vase life

Average

did you know

Each *Dahlia* "petal," like those on other flowers in the *Compositae* (daisy, sunflower) family, is a complete flower. *Dahlias* are actually composites of many individual flowers on one flower head.

lily

botanical name:
Lilium X *hybrida*

how to say it:
LIL-ee-um HIGH-bri-duh

common name:
Lily

classifications of hybrids:

- Asiatic hybrid lily
- Oriental hybrid lily
- LA (*longiflorum*/Asiatic) hybrid lily
- LO (*longiflorum*/Oriental) hybrid lily
- OT (Oriental/trumpet) hybrid lily

what they look like

Lilies have six-petaled trumpet-shaped blooms that flare open when fully developed. Size varies by type of hybrid.

colors

Red, pink, burgundy, orange, peach, salmon, yellow, white, cream, tan and bicolors

special care

THE RIGHT FOOD Hybrid lilies experience hormone imbalances when they are cut from their bulbs. These imbalances cause premature leaf yellowing, buds to fail to open, loss of color vibrancy and reduced vase lives. Use bulb-flower foods, which contain naturally occurring plant hormones, to help prevent those problems, and make sure your purchases are treated with hormone balancing solutions at the grower or wholesaler levels.

ETHYLENE SENSITIVE Yes

vase life

Average

did you know

Lily pollen will stain anything it touches, so remove all anthers immediately after each bloom opens. If pollen gets on fabric, brush it away lightly and gently with a fuzzy chenille stem (if a chenille stem is not available, use a soft cloth). Do not wet the fabric or touch the stain with your hands. If any pollen color remains, place the fabric outside in the sunshine until the stain disappears.

delphinium

del•phin•i•um

botanical name:
Delphinium spp.

how to say it:
del-FIN-ee-um

common names:
Belladonna *Delphinium*
Pacific hybrid *Delphinium* (shown)

what they look like

The backs of *Delphinium* florets are shaped like dolphins' noses. Belladonna hybrids are usually single flowered and have branched stems. Pacific hybrids have more densely clustered blooms—singles or doubles—and stems are nonbranched.

colors

Belladonna hybrids: light blue, dark blue and white. Pacific hybrids: light blue, dark blue, white, cream, mauve, lavender and purple, with white, brown or black centers.

did you know

Botanists used to include larkspurs in the *Delphinium* genus, but today, they are classified in a separate genus, *Consolida* (con-SAW-lid-uh). Care is the same as for *Delphiniums*.

special care

RECUT STEMS DAILY *Delphinium* stems tend to callous over quickly, so recut them daily, removing at least 1 inch, to maximize water uptake. Also, change the flower-food solution and clean containers at the same time.

SPLINT BROKEN STEMS *Delphinium* stems tend to be fragile. If a stem becomes bent or collapses, insert a wire or thin wood stake into the stem (depending on the diameter of the stem) to repair the problem. No wilting will occur if a stem has not been punctured or severed.

ETHYLENE SENSITIVE Yes

vase life

Average

lilac

li•lac

botanical name:
Syringa vulgaris

how to say it:
si-RIN-ga vul-GAW-ris

common name:
Lilac

what they look like

Lilacs' small star-shaped blossoms occur in dense pyramidal clusters atop tall woody stems. The flowers have a sweet, mild fragrance.

colors

Purple, lavender, mauve, pink and white

vase life

Average

did you know

The sap that exudes from the stems of freshly cut lilacs is said to reduce the vase life of other flowers, so don't mix lilacs with other flowers for at least six hours after processing.

special care

NO SMASHING Contrary to widespread belief, lilacs' woody stems should not be pounded or smashed; doing so damages the vascular system in the stems and inhibits water uptake. Instead, as with other flowers, recut the stems, and change the flower-food solution every other day.

HEAVY DRINKERS Lilacs are thirsty flowers, so check the solution level in containers daily.

WILTED BLOOMS Premature wilting is common with cut lilacs. It is not always due to microbes plugging the stem ends but rather to a substance the plants themselves produce, in response to ethylene, that blocks the midsections of the stems.

ETHYLENE SENSITIVE Yes

freesia

free•si•a

botanical name:
Freesia X *hybrida*
how to say it:
FREE-zhee-uh HIGH-bri-duh
common name:
None

what they look like

Freesia flower heads each comprise five to 10 fragrant trumpet-shaped florets and/or buds along the top, upper side of a curved stem. Each floret has six "petals," or segments. *Freesias* are available in single- and double-flowered varieties. Stems are thin, smooth and often branched. Foliage, which may not be included in cut flower bunches, is narrow and sword shaped.

colors

Red, pink, orange, rust/bronze, yellow, lavender, violet (purple), blue-violet, red-violet, white, cream and bicolors

special care

THE RIGHT FOOD AND WATER Store and arrange *Freesias* in bulb-flower-food solution prepared with cold nonfluoridated water. Fluoride can inhibit bloom development and opening and cause flower and leaf tip burn.

MOVE QUICKLY Sell *Freesias* within two days of receipt. Prolonged refrigeration of these flowers can cause chilling injury and diminish fragrance.

ETHYLENE SENSITIVE Yes

vase life

Average

did you know

Freesias are one of the most fragrant flowers although the intensity of the fragrance varies among varieties. Yellow, white and cream varieties are often more fragrant than other colors.

liatris

li•a•tris

botanical name:
Liatris spicata

how to say it:
lie-AT-tris spi-KAY-tuh

common names:
Gayfeather, Blazing star, Button snakeroot

what they look like

Liatrises form slender spikes of densely clustered flowers with needlelike petals, with the flowers encircling the stems. Stems are usually tall, thin, stiff and covered with thin spike- or lance-shaped leaves.

colors

Purple, lavender, red-violet and white

vase life

Average

did you know

Unlike most linear (spike) flowers, *Liatris* blossoms begin opening at the top of the stem and progress downward.

special care

LEAF YELLOWING AND REMOVAL
Liatris foliage can turn yellow quickly if the flowers become water stressed (dehydrated) and/or develop gray mold *(Botrytis)*. Be sure to remove all foliage that would be under water in storage or arrangement containers because it can rapidly deteriorate and contaminate the flower-food solution.

PROPER NUTRITION Although using properly proportioned flower-food solution is important with most flowers, it is particularly vital with *Liatrises*, to ensure the opening of most of the flowers on the spike.

ETHYLENE SENSITIVE No

gardenia

gar•de•nia

botanical name:
Gardenia jasminoides

how to say it:
gar-DEEN-yuh jaz-min-OY-deez

common name:
Cape jasmine

what they look like

Gardenia blooms are typically 3 inches in diameter although smaller blooms are available. These flowers have waxy petals and are usually dome shaped. In pristine condition, blooms are bright white and intensely fragrant.

color

White

vase life

Short

did you know

You can touch up bruises or blemishes on *Gardenias* gently with white or ivory floral spray paint on a cotton swab, typing correction fluid or even baby powder.

special care

NONDRINKERS *Gardenias* do not take up water after they are cut, so hydration and flower-food solutions are not necessary. Instead, spray the blooms with an antitranspirant, keep them sealed in their shipping boxes or air-tight bags, and store them in a floral cooler with high humidity (90 percent to 95 percent).

HANDLE WITH CARE *Gardenias* often yellow when exposed to air, and the petals bruise easily when touched. To minimize yellowing and bruising, spritz the blossoms with a solution of 90 percent water and 10 percent lemon juice prior to use, and keep them covered with wet cotton or facial tissue while working with them.

ETHYLENE SENSITIVE Yes

leucospermum

leu•co•sper•mum

botanical name:
Leucospermum spp.

how to say it:
lou-ko-SPUR-mum

common name:
Pincushion

what they look like

Pincushions have generally spherical flower heads made up of many tightly clustered flowers with long projecting styles, which give the flower heads the appearance of a pincushion. Stems are woody and crowded with short stiff leathery leaves.

colors

Red, red-orange, orange and yellow. Bicolors can occur as a result of styles that are a different hue than the flowers or that have tips or stripes of a different color.

did you know

Pincushions are members of the *Proteaceae* family and, therefore, are related to *Proteas*; however, they compose an entirely different genus than *Protea* and, technically, should not be referred to as pincushion *Proteas*.

special care

LEAF BLACKENING Be sure to use flower-food solution because the sugar in the solution can retard leaf blackening, which is common with these flowers. Low light and warm environments also contribute to leaf blackening, so provide plenty of light, even during refrigerated storage.

STORAGE TEMPS Although they are native to subtropical South Africa, pincushions are not chill sensitive and can be refrigerated at 33 F to 36 F.

FRESH TO DRY Pincushions can be air dried either by hanging them upside down in a cool, dry, airy, dark room or by leaving them in dry arrangement containers.

ETHYLENE SENSITIVE No

vase life

Average

gerbera

ger•ber•a

botanical name:
Gerbera jamesonii
how to say it:
GUR-bur-uh jaym-SO-nee-eye
common names:
Transvaal daisy, Barberton daisy, African daisy, Veldt daisy

what they look like

Gerberas' daisylike blooms are available in three sizes: *miniature* (2-3 inches in diameter); *standard* (3-5 inches in diameter); and *giant* (5-6 inches in diameter).

colors

Virtually every hue imaginable except for blue-green, blue and blue-violet. Centers can be yellow, green, brown, black or dark red/red-violet.

vase life

Average

did you know

Placing only the stem ends into water in storage containers can extend *Gerberas*' vase life. The furry stems promote bacterial growth, and shallow water will help prevent that from happening.

special care

KEEP THEM STRAIGHT To keep the stems from collapsing (called "conking"), suspend the flower heads through a mesh support or shipping tray, over the opening of their storage container, so the stems hang straight into the flower-food solution without touching the bottom of the container. You also can wire the stems or place them inside straws to keep them straight.

WATCH OUT FOR GERMS Change the flower-food solution and clean the storage containers every day because bacteria-contaminated water is particularly harmful to *Gerberas*, causing their stems to clog.

ETHYLENE SENSITIVE No

leucadendron

leu • ca • den • dron

botanical name:
Leucadendron spp.

how to say it:
lou-kuh-DEN-dron

common names:
Conebush (all)
Silver tree (*L. argenteum* only)

what they look like

In general, flower heads are composed of stiff colorful bracts surrounding a conelike flower (female) or inconspicuous flower (male). Thin woody stems are covered with leathery, closely packed leaves.

Silver tree *(L. argenteum)* has soft feathery green leaves covered in silvery silken pubescence (fine, short hairs).

colors

Red, burgundy, yellow, green and bicolors, with red, yellow, green and silver cones

did you know

Until their flower heads came to be appreciated for their own unique beauty, *Leucadendrons* were largely used in Europe as backing material in floral arrangements.

special care

WATER SUPPLY *Leucadendrons* are heavy drinkers, so monitor and replenish flower-food solution levels in storage containers frequently. Water stress (dehydration) can severely reduce these flowers' vase life.

LEAF BLACKENING Use flower-food solution because the sugar in the solution can retard leaf blackening, which is common with these flowers. Low light and warm environments also contribute to leaf blackening, so provide plenty of light, even during refrigerated storage.

STORAGE TEMPS Although *Leucadendrons* are native to subtropical South Africa, they are not chill sensitive and can be refrigerated at 33 F to 36 F.

ETHYLENE SENSITIVE No

vase life

Long

gladiolus

glad•i•o•lus

botanical name:
Gladiolus spp.
how to say it:
glad-ee-OH-lus
common names:
Sword lily, Corn flag

what they look like

Large-flowered *Gladioli* typically have 10 to 16 funnel-shaped blooms (and buds) per stem while miniature (butterfly) *Gladioli* usually have no more than seven. All blooms often have ruffly petal edges, and miniature *Gladioli* blooms often have blotched colorations. *Gladioli* leaves are sword shaped and are enwrapped around the stem ends and each other.

colors

Red, pink, burgundy, orange, peach, salmon, yellow, lime green, lavender, purple and bicolors

special care

THE RIGHT WATER Prepare flower-food solution with nonfluoridated water. *Gladioli* are extremely sensitive to fluoride, which causes deterioration of petal edges, failure of blooms to develop and open, and "burning" of the bud sheath.
CURVED TIPS *Gladioli* are geotropic (affected by gravity), so store them vertically and refrigerate them at 33 F to 35 F to prevent flower tips from curving.
ETHYLENE SENSITIVE Yes

vase life

Average

did you know

The term "gladiola" is often—but mistakenly—used as a common name for *Gladiolus*, which can sound like "gladiolas." In formal English, "gladiola" and "gladiolas" are not recognized words. The preferred plural of *Gladiolus* is *Gladioli*.

kangaroo paw

kan•ga•roo paw

botanical name:
Anigozanthos spp.

how to say it:
an-ee-go-ZAN-thos

common name:
Kangaroo paw

what they look like

Kangaroo paws produce clusters of woolly, tubular blossoms atop thin branching stems. The blooms have reflexed lips and resemble kangaroo toes. Foliage is long, narrow and grasslike, and occurs at the base of the plants/stems.

colors

Red, pink, burgundy, red-orange, orange and yellow as well as bicolors including red/green, yellow/green, yellow/orange, red/black and green/black

vase life

Average

did you know

Anigozanthos manglesii (the red/green species) is the state floral emblem of Western Australia. It appears on the crest of all government departments.

special care

STORAGE TEMPS Kangaroo paws are somewhat chill sensitive; therefore, they should be stored between 36 F and 40 F.

WATER STRESS These flowers easily become dehydrated, so process them as soon as they arrive in your store, and dip or place the stem ends into a hydration solution, prior to placing them into flower-food solution, to help them rehydrate quickly. Make sure containers always have plenty of flower-food solution.

FUNGAL INFECTION Although kangaroo paws require lots of water (flower-food solution), be sure to keep the blooms dry to prevent the development of *Botrytis* (gray mold).

ETHYLENE SENSITIVE No

godetia

go•de•tia

botanical names:
Clarkia amoena, syn. *Godetia*

how to say them:
CLARK-ee-uh a-MOY-nuh
go-DEE-she-uh

common names:
Satin flower, Farewell-to-spring

what they look like

Godetia's azalealike blooms are funnel-shaped and occur in clusters of four to eight at stem ends. Flower forms can be either single or double. Stems are densely covered with oval or lance-shaped leaves.

colors

Pink, rose, lavender, salmon, peach and white. Most have bicolored petals.

vase life

Average

did you know

These flowers are native to California, and the botanical name *Clarkia* was given in honor of Captain William Clark (1770-1838) of the Lewis and Clark expedition.

special care

LEAF YELLOWING AND REMOVAL
Godetia foliage often turns yellow quickly, and there is little that can be done about it at the retail level. It is important, though, to leave foliage on the stems (above water only) during storage. You can remove the leaves just prior to arranging these flowers.

STORAGE TEMPS Some cut flower authorities disagree about the proper storage temperatures for *Godetias.* Several say these flowers can be refrigerated at 33 F to 36 F while others say the flowers are chill sensitive and should be stored in the 40-F-to-low-50s-F range.

ETHYLENE SENSITIVE Yes

iris

i•ris

botanical name:
Iris, Dutch hybrids

how to say it:
EYE-ris

common names:
Fleur-de-lis, Flag

what they look like

Irises are composed of six "petals": three outer petals (falls), which arch downward and outward, and three inner petals (standards), which are more upright. The blooms occur atop thin stems with swordlike leaves.

colors

Blue, violet, yellow and white. Most are bicolored, with yellow markings on the falls and/or with standards of different hues.

did you know

The fleur-de-lis has been the symbol of France since the sixth century. It also has been revered as a religious symbol and used in architecture and décor for centuries.

special care

PROMOTING OPEN BLOOMS *Irises* may not open if handled improperly or stored too long before selling. Bloom opening can be encouraged by slicing the two sheathing leaves surrounding the unopened blooms along their "seams" and gently thumping the bloom with a finger.

THE RIGHT FOOD The use of bulb-flower-food solution also can promote bloom opening. These solutions contain "replacement" hormones and have a lower concentration of sugar, which helps prevent leaf yellowing.

ETHYLENE SENSITIVE No

vase life

Short

heather

heath•er

botanical names:
Calluna spp., *Erica* spp.

how to say them:
ka-LOO-nuh, AIR-i-kuh

common names:
Heather, Heath

what they look like

There are many species of heather and heath, but, in general, they are spikes of tiny, densely clustered bell-shaped or tubular flowers. The woody stems have needlelike leaves.

colors

Pink, red, red-violet, lavender, purple and white

vase life

Average

did you know

Although *Calluna* (heather) and *Erica* (heath) are different genera, they are closely related, and the differences between them are virtually indistinguishable to anyone other than a horticulturist or botanist.

special care

OUT OF THE WATER Make sure the lower blooms remain above water in storage containers and arrangements. This can require using shallow containers with low water levels; however, because these flowers are heavy drinkers, you must check the water level, especially in storage containers, at least once daily.

FRESH TO DRY Flowers and leaves dry out easily and/or often drop prematurely. This is normal, and there is little that can be done at the retail level to prevent it; however, additional value can be gained by air-drying these flowers in a warm, dry, airy, dark room.

ETHYLENE SENSITIVE No

hypericum

hy•per•i•cum

botanical name:
Hypericum spp.

how to say it:
high-PAIR-i-cum

common names:
St. John's wort, Tutsan

what they look like

Hypericum is primarily used in its fruited (seed capsule) form. The diminutive capsules, which resemble waxy berries, appear following flowering and grow in clusters atop branched, woody stems.

colors

Burgundy, red, pink, reddish brown, red-orange, salmon, yellow, green and white. The seed capsules ripen to mostly black to dark purple.

special care

STORAGE TEMPS *Hypericum* is slightly chill sensitive and should be refrigerated at 36 F to 41 F, for short periods only.

GLOVES RECOMMENDED The seed capsules may exude a reddish oil when crushed, so it may be advisable to wear latex gloves when processing *Hypericum*.

SOLUTION CONTAMINATION Like many woody-stemmed selections, *Hypericum* is likely to pollute its flower-food solution quickly, so recut the stems and change the solution at least every other day.

ETHYLENE SENSITIVE No

vase life

Long

did you know

St. John's wort is available as a "natural" or "herbal" over-the-counter remedy for all sorts of ailments, particularly anxiety and depression.

hyacinth

hy•a•cinth

botanical name:
Hyacinthus orientalis
how to say it:
high-a-SIN-thus or-ee-en-TAL-is
common names:
Hyacinth, Dutch hyacinth

what they look like

Hyacinths have small fragrant waxy bell-shaped blooms clustered to form flower spikes on the upper 4 to 6 inches of thick fleshy leafless stems.

colors

Blues, violets, pinks, red, peach, salmon, apricot, yellow and white

vase life

Short

special care

THE RIGHT FOOD Store and arrange hyacinths in flower-food solution formulated especially for bulb flowers.
THE RIGHT WATER Prepare bulb-flower solution with cold nonfluoridated water.
DO NOT RECUT Unlike most other flowers, recutting stems during processing is not advised. Leaving the basal plates (the white portion of the stem ends) intact improves water uptake and will extend vase life.
ETHYLENE SENSITIVE No

did you know

The genus name *Hyacinthus* is in honor of Hyakinthos, a youthful Spartan prince of great beauty in Greek mythology who was accidentally killed when he was hit in the head by a discus thrown by the Greek god Apollo.

hydrangea

hy•dran•gea

botanical name:
Hydrangea macrophylla
how to say it:
hy-DRAN-juh mak-row-FILL-uh
common name:
Hortensia

what they look like

Mophead *Hydrangeas* (shown) have small flat four-petaled florets that occur in dense large rounded clusters at stem ends. Lacecap *Hydrangeas* have center clusters of small round flowers, which resemble tiny berries, surrounded by larger four-petaled florets.

colors

Whites, pinks, lilacs, blues, greens and even browns as well as bicolors

did you know

Some *Hydrangea* colors are determined by soil acidity (blue) or alkalinity (pink) although new varieties are genetically engineered to achieve specific colors. Growers also use absorption dyes to alter *Hydrangea* colors.

special care

MOISTURE REQUIREMENTS *Hydrangeas* are heavy drinkers and wilt easily (*"Hydrangea"* comes from the Greek roots *"hydro/hydra,"* meaning water, which is an indication of the flower's water needs). Check the flower-food solution level daily, and change it and recut the woody stems (do not break, smash or crush the stems) every other day. Frequent misting is beneficial for flowers held at room temperature. Spraying blooms with antitranspirants also will extend cut *Hydrangeas'* vase life.

GROOMING TIP Pinch off florets as they fade.

ETHYLENE SENSITIVE Yes

vase life

Average